Healing Prayer

Healing Prayer

BARBARA LEAHY SHLEMON

Foreword by Francis MacNutt, O.P.

AVE MARIA PRESS
Notre Dame, Indiana 46556

Library of Congress Catalog Card Number: 75-36056
International Standard Book Number: 0-87793-108-9
© 1976 by Ave Maria Press. All rights reserved
Printed in the United States of America
Cover art by Sister Joan Marie Scheet, O.S.B.

I could not have written this book without the support and cooperation of my husband and children. May God bless them for their patience.

Barbara Leahy Shlemon is a registered nurse who obtained her degree from St. Francis Hospital School of Nursing in Evanston, Illinois. She has been a staff nurse in three hospitals from 1957 through 1969. Since then she has been a lecturer and teacher on the healing ministry in the Church and has worked with a healing ministry team under Father Francis MacNutt, O.P., which has been involved in healing prayer for many thousands of people throughout the United States and a number of other countries. Mrs. Shlemon is married and the mother of five children ages twelve through seventeen.

Contents

Foreword

I T WAS ON A memorable retreat in 1969
that I first met Mrs. Barbara Shlemon.
She had written to me after reading
that I was scheduled to give a charismatic
retreat at the Dominican Sisters' Mother-
house in Racine, Wisconsin, to say that
she would like to meet me since we knew
mutual friends, Rev. Tommy Tyson and
Mrs. Agnes Sanford, under whom she had
studied the healing ministry. I often
receive such letters offering to help out
on retreats, but when I met her at the
coffee break on Saturday morning I
realized at once that she was an extraor-
dinary person. When an urgent need
developed among many of the 90 re-

treatants to pray for inner healing I asked Barbara to help. As we prayed for so many brokenhearted people that evening, I realized in an even deeper way that God had wonderfully gifted Barbara with compassion together with a mighty power to heal.

Later, she filled me in and told me that she had begun praying for healing some years earlier when she was working as a registered nurse in a small hospital at a time when she knew of no other Roman Catholic who was doing such things. For years she was forced to walk a lonely way, faithful to her Church, but receiving what teaching was available on healing from Protestant friends.

That retreat began a marvelous team ministry (which included Sister Jeanne Hill, O.P., whom we also first met at that retreat), at a time when even some "charismatic" Catholic prayer groups were rejecting the notion of prayer for healing outside the sacraments as a Protestant intrusion. Fortunately, within a year this prejudice faded more and more until the June evening in 1974 when a healing service was held in the football stadium at Notre Dame with 20,000 Catholics present. As was only fitting, Barbara was part of the team that night praying the prayers of healing for the multitude, as she had so often in her prayer group and at countless retreats and conferences.

This team ministry has brought us to many countries of Latin America and, more recently, to England and Ireland. With the encouragement of her husband, Ben, she has developed a beautifully balanced ministry which extends to every form of prayer for healing, both physical and emotional. Over the past years I have seen God develop more and more of this gift of healing in Barbara—especially the word of knowledge—when no one knew humanly what to pray for. This gift has been a special help these past few years when she has been overwhelmed by multitudes of the sick asking for healing and there has been very little time to talk with each person.

Beyond all the ways that God has used Barbara in praying with people, she has a wonderful facility, too, in being able to explain things clearly and simply, especially in the area of inner (emotional) healing. This book is a reflection of all her years of teaching in Schools of Pastoral Care, and in workshops on healing that we have held in such places as Santiago (Chile), Cochabamba (Bolivia), Dublin (Ireland), Manchester (England), Notre Dame, Indiana, and New York City. Beyond that, though, this book contains the wisdom born of the experience of praying with thousands of people.

With the simplicity that will make her book easy for the ordinary lay person to understand, these pages also let the warmth shine through that animates her prayer and her presence when she speaks.

Francis S. MacNutt, O.P.

Introduction

ONE NIGHT IN 1964 the Lord taught me a lesson about his love which was to change my ideas about suffering and, ultimately, the course of my life. As a professional nurse, I was assigned to the evening shift of a medical-surgical ward in a small Midwest hospital. The report we received from the day shift showed one patient in a comatose condition who would probably expire during the night. The situation was particularly sad because the patient was a young mother of three small children who had put up a valiant fight for life during her stay in the hospital.

As I entered her room to check the flow

of her intravenous bottles, I was overcome with sorrow at the sight. The woman's weight had dropped to 90 pounds, most of it concentrated in fluid in her abdomen, which gave her the appearance of a nine-month pregnancy. Her arms and legs were like toothpicks; she had lost all the hair on her body, and jaundice colored her skin a deep yellow. She did not appear to respond to any kind of stimuli, and her breathing was very shallow and irregular.

I glanced at her husband across the room and wished there were words which could convey to him some comfort. The death of his wife seemed very near.

Back at the nurses' station I confessed my feelings of inadequacy to Harriet Saxton, the other nurse on duty with me. She agreed that the situation was grave but she didn't believe it was hopeless. I knew Harriet to be a devout Episcopalian with a deep faith that God really answered prayer. I felt, however, that she was being unrealistic in believing God could or would intervene in this case.

Undaunted by my skepticism, she

approached the husband with the suggestion that he contact his parish priest to anoint his wife with the sacrament of Extreme Unction. For many years this sacrament of anointing with oil was looked upon as a preparation for death, the final unction. Harriet explained that the recent Vatican Council had undertaken to return the concept of this sacrament to its original emphasis, the sacrament of the sick. It was to be administered as a means of healing.

The husband took a long while to consider this action and finally decided there was no other recourse. The priest who answered the call was at the hospital within minutes. An elderly man, pastor of the local Catholic church, he quietly read through the Latin ritual, pausing at intervals to apply the holy oil to the sick woman's body. He also brought the Holy Eucharist with him in the form of a small host, but the woman was in too deep a coma to accept it. The priest gently touched it to her lips and left the hospital.

The whole procedure had only taken

minutes, no visible changes had occurred in the patient's condition, and I went off duty that night thinking we had instilled false hope in a hopeless case. The next afternoon found me back on duty. As I walked past the dying woman's room, I glanced in and froze in my tracks. She was sitting up at the side of the bed sipping soup. I couldn't believe it! The day nurse walking past me said, matter-of-factly, "She took a turn for the better last night."

My initiation into the healing power of Jesus Christ had begun and I could hardly contain my curiosity about the subject. I began reading the scriptures and discovered the great number of gospel texts concerned with healings. It had never occurred to me that such phenomena could be possible in the 20th century.

Harriet invited me to accompany her to a prayer meeting in Wheaton, Illinois, where I could meet other Christians who understood God's power to heal. These charismatic meetings under the direction of Rev. Richard Winkler, an Episcopal priest, led me into the baptism of the Holy Spirit. The wonderful people who attended the prayer group were instrumental in teaching me the joy of walking in the Spirit.

They encouraged me to remain in the Roman Catholic Church and prayed with me that the renewal of God's Spirit would touch all people. Two years later, when new stirrings of the Spirit were experienced at Duquesne University, signaling the beginning of the Catholic charismatic renewal, I realized the wisdom of this counsel.

Over the years, the Lord has given me many opportunities to learn about the healing ministry from Christians with wide and varied prayer experiences. The books and teachings of Mrs. Agnes Sanford gave me confidence in my ability to be an instrument of God's healing love. Mrs. Sanford and her husband, Edgar, an Episcopal priest, established a School of Pastoral Care to teach ministers and professional people how to pray for the sick. Attending these schools and learning from ministers such as John L. Sanford, Francis Whiting, Morton Kelsey and Herbert Nabb has deepened my understanding of the gospel message on healing.

Since 1969, it has been a great privilege to work with Father Francis MacNutt, a Dominican priest from St. Louis, Missouri, and author of the book, **Healing** (Ave Maria Press, 1974). We have participated in team retreats, workshops and seminars throughout North and South America to teach others how to pray for healing.

The following chapters contain numerous references to holy scripture using texts from the **Jerusalem Bible.** I am not attempting to make a scholarly presentation of the word of God, but only wish to share some insights obtained through thoughtful reflection on the scriptures. I have interpreted these passages in the light of my own personal experiences with intercessory prayer during the past decade, conscious of the fact that my education is in medicine, not theology.

The medical profession has long been skeptical of the spiritual approach to healing because it has been characterized by zealous evangelists admonishing people to "claim your healing" and "throw away your medicine." Most doctors are so offended by these narrow-minded methods that they dismiss all healing prayer as religious fanaticism.

I believe it is possible and necessary to integrate the physical and spiritual care of people in order to bring about true wholeness. There is no doubt in my mind that the Lord works through natural means such as the competence of a surgeon, the wisdom of a diagnostician and the benefits obtained by medication and therapy. However, I am deeply concerned that those of us involved in caring for the sick have failed to recognize the importance of the spiritual dimension. Even many hospitals founded by religious orders have lost sight of their original commitment to the body, mind and spirit of individuals.

This book is not written as a complete

guide to praying for the sick. There is so much to learn and each of us has only a portion of the vision. It **is** written with a fervent prayer that the reader will be stimulated to discover his own ability to become a channel for the healing love of Jesus Christ.

The Lord clearly directed me to a full-time ministry of healing after I spent many agonizing months seeking his will for my life. The conflict between my deep desire to care for the sick as a professional nurse and my equally strong desire to concentrate on the spiritual dimension of wholeness, was finally resolved one night.

I had worked more than an hour overtime in order to finish the charting which had been neglected while I busied myself praying with patients. As I drove into the driveway of our home and turned off the ignition, the presence of the Lord seemed to fill the entire car. His closeness triggered a torrent of tears as I cried out my frustrations and confusions concerning my vocation.

Deep within my heart I felt Jesus asking

whether I were willing to put away my uniform and cap and follow him. My whole being resisted the idea with numerous arguments, such as, "There is such a shortage of nurses," and "What about the time, energy and money that went into my education?"

The voice within me persistently requested an answer. Was I willing to put aside my chosen career and embark on a new journey? It seemed as if I sat in the car for hours while the battle raged inside me. Finally, I tearfully abandoned myself to the Lord, agreed to resign my hospital position, and was flooded with an overwhelming sense of peace. No lightning bolts flashed through the sky, just a quiet knowing that I had done the right thing.

It was three years from the time of that decision until I discovered God directing me to teach others to pray for the sick. In my wildest imaginings, I would never have considered such a ministry and still feel woefully inadequate for the task. I've come to recognize this as an asset since it compels me to rely solely on the guidance of the Holy Spirit in all things.

God continues to reveal his truths to mere children and I am constantly surprised by his teachings. The past several years have provided ample confirmation that I was on the path God charted for me. I have had opportunities to observe countless persons come into a new relationship with the Lord through his healing touch. A recent letter from a Catholic nun who was healed during a Camp Farthest Out healing service, illustrates this point.

> It is so wonderful to be free from the misery of pain, double vision and vertigo which has plagued me for six years, plus three surgeries, all of them unsuccessful. I am sure life will take on new meaning for me now. Visiting the sick and comforting their relatives is my new job.

God released her from the bondage of physical suffering and she is truly a new person. Reports of such healings are being received throughout the world with more and more frequency.

What about those people who retain their infirmities despite repeated prayer efforts? There are an infinite number of reasons why people are not healed and only our Father in heaven really knows the answer to that question. Years of experience have taught me to stop expending so much energy asking, "Why aren't they all healed?" and to realize that the problem is too complex for my mind. I've learned to direct my efforts toward praying for the sick, leaving the results up to the Creator who is still very much in charge of his universe. I have absolutely no doubts that the Lord wants wholeness for all of us, but he will bring it about in his way and in his time.

The Book of Revelation describes for us the "new heaven and the new earth" where God "will wipe away all tears from (our) eyes; there will be no more death and no more mourning or sadness. The world of the past has gone" (Rv 21:1-4).

Until that day comes, we have the responsibility to keep the light of Jesus Christ burning on the earth. Our prayers can do much to hasten his return.

Chapter 1

Who Has the Gift of Healing?

And these signs shall follow all who believe,
they shall lay their hands upon the sick, who
will recover.

Mark 16:17

JESUS PERFORMED MANY WORKS of
healing as he walked among men upon
the earth. Whenever he encountered
people who were suffering, he alleviated
their pain and restored them to
wholeness.

Most Christians do not have difficulty
believing that the Lord possessed the gifts
of healing necessary to mend a sick body.
After all, Jesus is God Incarnate, and God
can do anything.

We read the scriptural accounts of healing miracles and we wish Jesus were here to cure the sick in our day and age. With more and more hospitals being built, doctors unable to keep up with the needs of an increasing population, and many illnesses still considered incurable, we could certainly use this charism of healing.

The Good News is, we **do** have the healing love of Jesus Christ with us today. The gifts of healing as manifested by the Lord have been delegated to each person who accepts Jesus as his Savior, believing him to be the Son of God.

Before he was crucified, Jesus said to his disciples, "Whoever believes in me will perform the same works as I do myself, he will perform even greater works, because I am going to the Father" (Jn 14:12). Jesus was telling the disciples that ministering to the blind, the halt and the lame was not going to stop when he was no longer visible. The commission to carry on the healing work was given to "whoever believes" in him. The works would be even greater because they would no longer be performed by one man, but by everyone who professes Jesus as Lord.

Jesus made us extensions of himself in order that multitudes of people could be touched and cured by his love. He has no hands to lay on the sick but our hands. If, as Christians, we really believe the Lord dwells within us, then it should not come as a surprise that we can pray for the sick and they will be healed. We merely provide the vehicle through which the love of God can shine forth.

Christians are accustomed to thinking that the gift of healing is reserved for certain individuals who receive a supernatural "call" from God to go forth and heal. We read the lives of the saints and find it difficult or impossible to emulate their heroic acts of holiness and piety. Therefore, we conclude that we couldn't possibly imitate their works of healing. We equate miracles with shrines like Lourdes and Fatima and seldom consider that Jesus expected us to do such works. If it is true that God "does not have favorites" (Acts 10:34), then we must each seek to develop our relationship with God to its fullest potential.

A common excuse for not exercising the gift of healing is, "I'm not worthy." There is a feeling of inadequacy in each of us which makes us think we have a long way to go before God can use us. We draw back from commitment until we can, somehow, get ourselves completely pure and holy, then we'll be ready to serve the Lord.

The Good News is that Jesus Christ came to save us "while we were still sinners" (Rm 5:8), and he wants to use us with all our weaknesses, inadequacies and impurities. As long as we remain aware of our faults, then we must rely totally on his strength, goodness and holiness.

The people who are the most effective in the healing ministry are those who are painfully aware of their limitations, yet put themselves at the disposal of God. We are of little value to the Lord when we are self-reliant and dependent upon our own strength. Feelings of unworthiness do not remove our responsibility for exercising the healing ministry, but should make us more sensitive instruments for the Lord's use.

After I had witnessed the young woman healed through the Anointing of the Sick, I began to experiment with prayer. I reasoned that, if a sacrament could produce such dramatic results, perhaps my feeble prayers might be sufficient to comfort some of the patients. Therefore, I decided to look for opportunities to pray with the sick who were in my care. I had no previous training in prayer techniques, but I did have a deep desire to relieve suffering and see people healed. There was a willingness to be a fool for Christ if it could help someone.

My first opportunity came in the person of an elderly man who was in an advanced stage of carcinoma. He was in great pain, requiring heavy doses of narcotics, constantly retching and vomiting. One afternoon, as I was administering his injection, I asked if he would like me to say a prayer with him. He clutched my hand very tightly and said, "Would you please ask God to help me?" I said a brief word about God loving him enough to die for him and we recited the Lord's Prayer together. The old gentleman fell into a quiet, restful sleep and I left the room. He lived for several more weeks before he went to be with Jesus, but he never needed another narcotic nor had any further episodes of vomiting. Could it have been a coincidence or the power of suggestion at work in this situation? The explanation seemed secondary to the fact that a human being was relieved of his misery. I decided to continue experimenting.

A few days later, we admitted an 83-year-old man who was scheduled for prostate surgery. His doctor was concerned that the operation might be too great a strain for the man's already weakened heart so it was with much reluctance he agreed to perform the necessary surgery. The night before the operation, I went into the patient's room and said a quiet prayer asking Jesus to heal the enlarged prostate. The hospital orderly wheeled him to the operating room at eight o'clock the next morning and brought him back at eight thirty. No surgery was performed because the prostate was no longer enlarged.

These answered prayers captured the attention of June Stewart, a licensed practical nurse assigned to work with Harriet and me. She conceived the idea of gathering together an intercessory prayer group, made up of hospital personnel, who would pray for the needs of the staff and the patients.

On our 3 P.M. to 11 P.M. shift, the only available time for such a meeting was during the evening coffee break. And so it was that six people began to gather together for prayer every evening in an unused operating room. Few people outside the group knew what was being done, but the entire hospital seemed to benefit from those quiet moments of meditation.

During this time we would often pray for our more critical patients and their families. Sometimes this prayer brought about definite improvement in physical condition; sometimes it gave people courage and confidence to undergo surgery; sometimes it conferred added strength for a dying patient and his family; always prayer seemed to be a positive influence which introduced inner peace.

There was no way to prove that prayer was a factor in aiding these situations, but we discovered that "coincidences" seemed to happen more frequently after we petitioned the Lord.

The teachings of Jesus certainly emphasize the importance of asking, so for several months the hospital prayer group continued to carry out the directive, "Ask in my name. . . ."

Chapter 2
Guidance

Whatever you ask for in my name I will do, so that the Father may be glorified in the Son. If you ask for anything in my name, I will do it.

John 14:14

"IF GOD IS ALL-KNOWING then he knows my needs and I don't have to ask him for anything." This rationale is used by many people who think that prayer is a lazy approach to life's problems. "God helps those who help themselves," they say, oblivious to the fact that Jesus Christ came to help those who could not help themselves. This doesn't imply that we sit back and passively wait for our Lord to handle every detail, but it does teach us to allow Jesus to become a partner in working out the answers to our prayers.

Jesus told his disciples, "Your Father knows what you need before you ask him" (Mt 6:8), then he went on to teach them the Lord's Prayer so they would know how to ask. Our relationship was not to be a passive dependence on the Father's love but an actively cooperative effort in obtaining our "daily bread." The Lord provides for many of our needs without our petitioning for his help. Yet he often expects us to be specific in our asking so our "joy will be complete" (Jn 16:24).

We have been given free will; therefore, the Lord doesn't take us for granted. He won't violate the sanctity of our individuality.

When the two blind men shouted to Jesus, "Lord! Have pity on us, Son of David," he asked them, "What do you want me to do for you?" He didn't automatically assume that they wanted to be healed. Only after they requested, "Lord, let us have our sight back," did he touch their eyes and restore them.

How many desires of our heart go unanswered because we fail to ask? We also fail to take into account the second part of the Lord's teaching which admonishes us to "ask in my name." This doesn't mean that we tack the name of Jesus Christ to the end of all our prayers like some magic formula for success. Jesus was addressing himself to Jews who understood that a person's name signified his destiny, personality and character. Jewish parents took great care in naming their children because the name would signify the direction and attitude of their lives. There are scriptural references to the Lord's changing individuals' names after they had had a spiritual experience which altered their life-style; for example, Sarah, Abraham, Peter, Paul. When Jesus tells us to ask "in his name," he is teaching us to pray in his personality and character. He wants us to develop the same kind of intimate relationship he had with the

Father so that our prayers will always be answered.

This kind of relationship cannot be achieved overnight but requires us to continually immerse ourselves in the personality of Jesus until we become conformed to his image and likeness. Daily scripture reading, particularly from the gospels, time for personal and corporate prayer, and reading from good devotional material can aid us in realizing this goal.

We often fail to ask for God's help because we believe our needs too trivial for his consideration. This limits the Lord's involvement in our lives since we pray only during crises situations. If we **don't** see the Lord answering prayers for the little things, it will be difficult to trust in him when disaster is upon us. Faith builds with experience and needs to be strengthened through practice.

Jesus also stated that our prayers would be answered "so that the Father would be glorified in the Son." This can only occur if we are seeking to do the Father's will through our intercessions. Many times our prayer requests don't bear fruit because we neglected to discover what the Lord wanted in the situation. We assume that his will is the same as ours without first asking for his guidance.

I prayed for many years that my husband would become a Roman Catholic and join me in the ministry of healing. It never entered my thoughts that our Lord might have something else in mind. When nothing seemed to happen in this regard, I finally realized that God had not been consulted and I prayed for his guidance. The Holy Spirit taught me that I was praying for the wrong person to be changed because I was the one who needed the transforming. There were many areas in my life where I was not being submissive, forgiving and loving. When I began asking the Lord to make me a better Christian wife and mother, the way opened up for my husband, Ben, to take some positive spiritual steps which eventually enabled him to join the Church.

Seeking the Lord's guidance is an essential factor in healing prayer. We need to spend time listening to the directions of the Holy Spirit for our prayers to become more effective. We begin by asking, "Lord, what do **you** want to do in this situation?" and then pray in accordance with his leading. It takes practice to develop this kind of "listening ear," but the more we test these inner messages and prove their accuracy, the more we will be able to rely on them. We might ask for the "gift of ears" as well as the gift of tongues.

Our prayer group was once asked to pray for a young boy who was dying of kidney failure. We joined together and asked Jesus to touch his body and restore it to health. Several prophesies were given that he was being healed, but the hospital report the next day showed further deterioration in his condition. We again gathered for prayer, but this time asked the guidance of the Holy Spirit and what he wanted for this youngster. One of the women in the group received an inner feeling that the boy's mother was an obstacle to the flow of God's power. She discerned that the mother's fears and anxieties were so great that they created a spiritual barrier between him and the Lord. She suggested, therefore, that we pray for the mother rather than the son.

We interceded in this direction, asking God to give the mother an overwhelming sense of his presence so she could believe the Lord's love for her child was greater than her love could ever be. She later reported to us that she received a powerful anointing of love while she sat at the boy's bedside and she knew Jesus was in the room. As she praised God and thanked him for touching her son, he began to move around in the bed. Moments later, when the nurse came to check his condition, she was amazed that his vital signs had returned to normal. Within three weeks he left the hospital and returned to school.

Every situation requires its own unique spiritual direction. The gospel narratives show us that Jesus did not follow a set pattern in his healing ministry but treated each request for help differently. One paralytic is told to take up his bed and walk and another is advised that his sins are forgiven. Jesus laid his hands on one blind man to restore his sight and he applied a mixture of mud and spittle to heal another.

It appears that Jesus treated each person as an individual when he answered their needs. We should also develop this kind of attitude for our prayer intentions.

Chapter 3
How Should We Pray?

Jesus answered, "Have faith in God. I tell you solemnly, if anyone says to this mountain, 'Get up and throw yourself into the sea,' with no hesitation in his heart but believing that what he says will happen, it will be done for him. I tell you therefore: everything you ask and pray for, believe that you have it already, and it will be yours."

Mark 11:23-25

JESUS GAVE SOME firm guidelines to his disciples concerning intercessory prayer. This passage from St. Mark illustrates the attitude of faith he expected from his followers who were seriously seeking answers to their petitions. Years of experience have convinced me that our prayer life will be more richly blessed if we follow the rules Jesus laid down.

Prayers for physical needs, emotional balance, spiritual renewal become more effective when we apply these simple principles to our asking.

The scripture passage describes Jesus and the disciples on the road into Jerusalem. They had traveled this way the previous day when our Lord had commanded the fig tree, "May no one ever eat fruit from you again." Peter expressed amazement that the tree had "withered away" during the night and Jesus uses the incident as a teaching.

The Lord's first direction states, "Have faith in God. . . ." The word "faith" can often be a stumbling block to Christians because we view it as some abstract spiritual component that will somehow add magic to our prayers. This idea is reinforced by "claim your healing" ministers who continually exhort people to have faith as they pray over them and accuse them of a lack of faith if the answer is not forthcoming. This method puts an unfair burden of responsibility upon the person seeking help because he is often too spiritually depressed or physically weak to have faith in anything. Telling him he lacks faith usually adds guilt to an already desperate situation.

Sometimes the responsibility for believing rests with the person doing the praying rather than the one asking for help. The healing of the paralytic in Luke 5:17 is such an example. The four friends were unable to maneuver the man on his mat through the crowd. Undaunted, they carried him to the top of the house where they removed the loose tiles and lowered him to the feet of Jesus. Seeing **their** faith he said, "My friend, your sins are forgiven you." Perhaps nothing is said about the faith of the sick man because he was so wounded in body and spirit that he ceased to believe he could be cured. Jesus was able to appropriate the faith of his friends to bring wholeness to his life.

We cannot command faith into a person. It is an attitude which develops as we learn of the great love the Father has for each of us. Whenever we read the word "faith" in the scripture, it is helpful to insert the word "trust" to gain better understanding of the message. . . . If we trust someone, we believe he has our best interests at heart so we are not continually questioning his desire for our welfare.

I ask a friend to care for our children over a weekend so I trust her to look after them with love and concern. I do not repeatedly beg her to be certain that they get enough sleep or plead with her to feed them at mealtimes. It never enters my mind to consider such a lack of love from a friend.

Yet we often approach our Father in heaven with this kind of anxiety and fear. We beg him to see the seriousness of our problems or we plead with him for the healing of our loved ones as if we were attempting to overcome his destructive will. We have become so caught up in the mentality which assigns the cause for every disaster to the will of God that we fail to realize that Jesus became incarnate to show us the true personality of the Deity.

Jesus told us, "The Son can do nothing

by himself; he can do only what he sees
the Father doing; and whatever the Father
does the Son does too" (Jn 5:19). If Jesus
is the visible manifestation of the Father's
concern for us, then God's love is very
great indeed.

To "have faith in God" means to trust
that the Father's will for us is much more
wonderful than we can possibly imagine.
Our attitude, as we approach him in
prayer, needs to be childlike in simplicity.
We should believe the Lord wants to
answer our prayer requests more than we
want to ask for them. Only then can we
trust the answers to our petitions to be in
the best interests of everyone concerned.

The next requirement the Lord set
forth in his teaching is: "If anyone says to
this mountain. . . ." It is important to note
that Jesus does not tell us to ask the
Father in heaven to speak to the
mountain but he teaches that authority for
moving the mountain rests within us. This
recalls the accounts of creation in the
Book of Genesis, "God blessed them,
saying to them, 'Be fruitful, multiply, fill

the earth and **conquer** it. Be masters of the fish of the sea, the birds of heaven and all living animals upon the earth' '' (Gn 1:28).

As the highest form of life on earth, God gave man dominion over all of his creation. This gives us the authority to correct those areas of nature which are not in harmony with God's perfection. Jesus did this with the fig tree and he expects us to do the same whenever we encounter a disruption in the earth.

Perhaps we will never be in a position to need to move a mountain, but that kind of authority can be exercised in other ways. Occasionally, I have asked for guidance when praying for a sick person and received the impression that I was to command the illness to depart and it has complied. Just as our Lord rebuked the fever of Peter's mother-in-law and she got up from her bed (Mt 8:14), so we are sometimes guided to take authority over sickness.

This was illustrated one evening after we had begun holding regular weekly prayer meetings in our homes. A young woman requested prayer prior to undergoing surgery for a lump in the breast. We asked Jesus to surround her with his love and remove the terrifying anxiety she was experiencing. Then we spoke to the cells in her body which were not acting in a healthy, creative manner and told them to stop their erratic behavior. The lump disappeared almost immediately and, after examination, her doctor canceled the surgery.

When our son, Steve, was eight years old he fell from the upper bunk of his bed and lay on the floor screaming with pain in his right arm. X rays showed a pathological fracture of his arm which was not caused by the accident but due to an unusually large bone cyst which had been developing for some time. The cyst, growing inside the bone of his upper arm, had reduced it to the fragility of an eggshell.

The two orthopedic specialists who examined Steve impressed us with the seriousness of his condition. He would be in a cast from his neck to his waist for at least six months, then in a sling for another extended period. We were advised to "teach him how to play chess" because physical activity would aggravate the condition.

Our prayer group prayed over Steve, asking Jesus to accelerate this healing process. We encouraged him to speak to the cells in his arm, asking them to fill in all the empty places with strong, bony tissue. After six weeks the cast was removed and X rays taken to determine proper alignment.

The physician seemed somewhat incredulous as he compared the latest X rays to the originals and could find no evidence of a fracture or a bone cyst. No further treatment was necessary and when I asked about limiting Steve's activity, he replied, "A kid who heals that fast can do anything he pleases."

Perhaps talking to a mountain and expecting it to move isn't so farfetched after all.

Jesus also teaches us, "Everything you

ask and pray for believe that you have it already and it will be yours." How can we manifest that kind of belief when we see the suffering, hopelessness and despair in a situation? We are asked to believe in our hearts that the needs we are praying for are already taken care of so it can be done. This is the portion of the prayer of faith which requires us to use our creative imaginations. Because we live in a culture which demands rational and scientic data to explain every phenomenon, we have a tendency to disregard as unimportant anything we cannot touch, taste, see or smell. Therefore, we oftentimes fail to recognize the promptings of the Holy Spirit which come through dreams, visions, prophetic words and imagination because we have not learned to trust our spiritual sensors.

The use of our imagination in prayer can aid us in "believing that we have it already." A report in the **New York Times** (August, 1973) quotes Dr. Walter Chase, director of research and head of the department of basic and visual science at

the Southern California College of
Optometry in Fullerton, as saying, "The
things one sees in the mind's eye are as
real, in one sense, as the things one sees
through a window." He goes on to
explain that there is not much physio-
logical difference between the signals
that are activated by the mind's eye and
the ones that are activated by the eye
itself.

Dr. Chase's experiments are showing
that the same physical mechanism is at
work when we think we see something
happen and when we actually do see the
thing take place. The imagination is not a
passive component of our beings but can
become an extremely active ingredient in
our prayers.

When the Holy Spirit guides me to pray
for someone who is ill, I picture Jesus
touching the person, making him whole,
healthy and strong, and thank the Lord
that this is taking place even when there
is no visible evidence of change. I continue to hold on to this picture of wholeness until it becomes a reality, praising

and thanking God that the answer will be forthcoming.

A woman once asked me to pray for her father who was dying of emphysema. After explaining this method of believing prayer, she understood the teaching but had great difficulty using her imagination. Her solution was to find a photograph of her dad taken when he was strong and healthy. She placed the picture above the kitchen sink and, as she washed her dishes, she would thank our Lord for restoring her father's body, mind and spirit. He was soon discharged from the hospital and able to return to work.

Jesus can truly become active in a situation when we stop wishing him to correct the problem and start believing that he is already at work. The letter to the Hebrews tells us, "Faith can . . . prove the existence of the realities that at present remain unseen" (Heb 11:1). Our intercessory prayers manifest this kind of faith when we begin to thank the Lord for his merciful love even though we see no external evidence of it.

Chapter 4

Forgiveness

I give you a new commandment, love one another as I have loved you.

John 13:34

JESUS DID NOT merely suggest that we were to love one another, he made it a new commandment. There was to be no more conjecture on the nature of love because God became a human being in order to show us how it should be done. His love for us was total, encompassing everyone, including his enemies. He denounced the scribes and Pharisees in his teachings but he did not exclude them from the benefits of his redemptive act. In the midst of the agonizing suffering of his crucifixion he blessed his persecutors, "Father, forgive them; they do not know what they are doing" (Lk 23:34).

Does our love for others measure up to the example of Jesus Christ or are we continuing to hold on to hurt feelings, resentment, or anger toward other people?

There is nothing that will impede our ability to pray for ourselves or for others more than the unwillingness to forgive. It acts as an invisible barrier between us and the Father which prohibits his blessings from being showered upon us or the ones for whom we pray.

Jesus taught us, "When you stand in prayer, forgive whatever you have against anybody, so your Father in heaven may forgive your failings too" (Mk 11:25). We cannot have the fullness of God's love for ourselves or for others so long as we refuse to make an act of forgiveness toward those who have wronged us.

"But I have forgiven that person," we argue, "I just don't like to be around him."

True forgiveness includes forgetting the wrongdoing and a willingness to communicate with the other party when circumstances bring us together.

"If you knew the terrible things he did to me you wouldn't expect me to forgive him," we state as our reason for holding on to resentment. Of course, the trauma of the situation was extremely painful or it would not have caused so much heartache. However, the commandment to love one another does not make allowances for the degree of pain we received but insists that we love anyway.

I once prayed with a woman suffering with a chronic bladder infection. She had sought relief through many forms of medication but the discomfort persisted. Several people had unsuccessfully prayed with her for healing, so I prayed for guidance asking the Lord the best way to minister to this woman. I felt led to inquire about her past which she graphically described as being in hell. Her husband had deserted the family for another woman leaving her the sole support of three young children. The bitterness in her voice as she related the story told me much more than the words ever could.

We talked about the lack of love being an obstacle to healing and I asked if she were willing to make an act of forgiveness toward her husband. At first she was very defensive, using many arguments to substantiate her right to hate this man who had caused them so much misery. As we talked she gradually came to realize that the hatred was hurting her far more than it was punishing him. I asked her to pray a blessing for her husband, forgiving him for neglecting her and the children. Then we prayed the prayer of faith, asking Jesus to touch her body and heal it. Several weeks later I received a letter stating that, not only had the physical problem disappeared, but she had experienced a new feeling of joy in her life.

Sometimes we need to repeatedly practice this act of forgiveness when we live or work with someone who makes life miserable for us. Jesus told Peter that he was to forgive those who wronged him, "seventy times seven times" (Mt 18:22), which means we do not keep a record of the number of transgressions committed against us. Therefore, we occasionally find ourselves in a situation where we have to continually say, "Lord, I forgive this person who keeps hurting me. Let me see him as you see him and love him as you love him." If we make a conscious effort to allow the love of Jesus to flow through us to another person, it begins to have a healing effect on the whole situation.

After I began to understand the beneficial effects of prayer in the recovery of my patients, I spent more time ministering to them spiritually than caring for them physically. This did not endear me to the medical staff of the hospital. One doctor in particular gave me a hard time and availed himself of every opportunity to chide me for "getting religion" and becoming a "Holy Roller." We had been close friends and, since he was unable to understand the changes in me, he resorted to sarcastic remarks which left deep wounds in me.

The simplest way of dealing with the situation was to avoid him whenever possible, but I realized this was not a solution. Therefore, I began applying the forgiving love of Jesus Christ whenever we had an encounter. I knew my love was not sufficient, but there was no doubt in my mind that God loved this man unconditionally. Each time he would begin to harass me, I would ask Jesus to fill me with his love so it could overflow onto the doctor. Our relationship gradually became less strained, the heckling stopped and we were able to develop our friendship again. Practicing this kind of forgiving love can sometimes require time and effort but the results are worth the struggle.

Once we make a decision to forgive the other person, then the channel is open for God's love to work and our prayers to be answered. It is important to remember that forgiveness is a decision, an act of our will which can be effective when we do not feel particularly loving toward another person. Once we decide to take the step and make an act of forgiveness in prayer, the spiritual mechanism is set in motion for our entire being to respond with love. If we sincerely desire to forgive, our feelings will eventually follow suit.

A young girl requested healing prayers for her body which had been maimed by rifle shots from a disgruntled neighbor. She had been hospitalized for many months and undergone surgery numerous times to repair the internal damage done to nearly every organ of her body. When we asked if she was willing to forgive her assailant, she replied very forcefully and very negatively against any such action. The person had caused too much heart-ache to her and her family and she would go to her grave hating him.

As I prayed for guidance from the Holy Spirit, I felt impressed to ask her if she could pray to become **willing to be willing** to forgive the neighbor. This was acceptable and she quietly made such a request. The peace which it brought to her spirit was instantaneous and, although her physical body has not been completely healed, she received the baptism of the Holy Spirit and a deep awareness of the presence of God in her life.

It is good practice during prayer time to

sit quietly and ask the Lord to bring to mind anyone whom we need to forgive. If a name comes to us we can ask the Holy Spirit to grant us the grace necessary to "see" this individual with the eyes of Jesus and to forgive him with the Lord's forgiving love. We can say a prayer of thanksgiving that Jesus will correct anything lacking in our human ability to love with his perfect love.

It is important to forgive people who have wronged us and equally necessary to ask forgiveness when we have offended another person. Jesus told us, "If you are bringing your offering to the altar and there remember that your brother has something against you, leave your offering there before the altar, go and be reconciled with your brother first, and then come back and present your offering" (Mt 5:23-25).

Sometimes we overlook this require-ment, not realizing that it can hinder the answer to our petitions. For several weeks, we received no answer to our prayers for a woman who was trying to find employment. She was the sole support for her teenage children and their financial situation was becoming desperate. One evening as we were praying with her, someone asked if she could recall anything which might be a block in the situation. Was there a person she needed to forgive or, perhaps, someone who needed to forgive her.

She remembered that her former employer had fired her because she gossiped about him to the office staff. There had been many hurt feelings and no effort made to reconcile the relationships. Early the next morning she walked into the man's office, apologized for her thought-less behavior and asked his forgiveness. He was understandably puzzled by the unexpected visit and cautiously accepted her apology. A few hours later, she received a phone call informing her that a job application she had written several weeks before had been accepted. Forgiveness opened the channel for God to answer.

If we are serious in the desire to seek

answers to our needs, then we have to be willing to fulfill God's conditions. Every promise in the bible carries with it a corresponding requirement which the believer is expected to fulfill. Jesus mentions forgiveness so often in his teachings that we ought to recognize the deep significance of this action.

The need to forgive and be forgiven also extends to our relationship with God. It is not uncommon for human beings to become upset with the Lord and there are many scripture passages which illustrate such an attitude. Moses cried out against God, "Why do you treat your servant so badly? Why have I not found favor with you, so you load on me the weight of all this nation? If this is how you want to deal with me, I would rather you killed me!" (Nm 11:12-15).

Several of the psalms (e.g., Pss 6, 13, 22, 77, 89) also express similar discontent with Divine Providence, therefore, I presume God is able to contend with our outbursts. We have a serious problem, however, when we allow our anger and resentment to block us from his love.

I once cared for a man who was furious with the Lord because, as he described it, "God killed my son in an auto accident." For many years, he refused to go to church or permit anyone in his family to discuss religion. He was hospitalized in the final stages of cancer of the bowel when we began to pray that he be reconciled with the Lord. His bitterness continued until the night before he died when he finally consented to a visit from the hospital chaplain. Later, he tearfully told his wife, "Honey, I feel such peace, why didn't I do this years ago?"

Occasionally our anger against God is so subtle that we are unaware of the fact that it is causing a lack of joy, an inability to pray, a lack of trust or a spirit of despair. Meditating on the passages in scripture where Jesus talked about the "Father" can help us to gain a better perspective on his great love. We can experience the answer to our Lord's prayer for us, "Father, Righteous One, the world has not known you, but I have known you, and these have known that you have sent me. I have made your name known to them and will continue to make it known, so that the love with which you loved me may be in them, and so I may be in them" (Jn 17:25-26).

Chapter 5

Healing Prayer and Group Meetings

I tell you solemnly once again, if two of you
agree to ask anything at all, it will be granted
to you by my Father in heaven. For where
two or three meet in my name, I shall be
there with them.

Matthew 18:20

PRIVATE PRAYER is important in the
development of spiritual life and it
needs to be practiced daily. However, the
phenomenal rise in the number of prayer
groups meeting throughout the world
gives evidence that Christians are also
heeding the Lord's call to collective
prayer. Jesus did not tell us why the
agreement of two or three people would

heighten the effectiveness of our prayers, but the experience of many groups seems to witness to this truth.

I have often received letters from people relating how they had interceded for a particular need for many years but saw little progress until they submitted the petition for group prayer. Sometimes the "death to self" involved in admitting our needs to others is a factor in opening the door. Most often it is the power exerted by the body of believers which makes the difference. When we gather to praise and worship the Lord, there seems to be a tangible current of divine energy flowing through the group which assures us of his presence.

This current of God's love provides the environment which enables us to communicate with the Father and with one another. The Lord's concern for us becomes a reality when it is reflected in the loving attitude of the brothers and sisters who join us in prayer. It is much easier for me to believe that God is interested in answering my needs when I feel the human concern of my friends.

We can contribute to this spiritually beneficial climate by our thoughtful consideration for other people. One way of conveying an interest in others is by becoming a good listener. Dr. Morton Kelsey of the Department of Graduate Studies at Notre Dame University and author of **Healing and Christianity** (Harper and Row, 1973) says, "50% of all psychiatry is non-judgmental, loving, listening."

There is no greater gift we can give others than our undivided attention and loving interest in what they are saying.

Listening can also enable us to develop deeper attitudes of compassion and understanding. The word "compassion" means "to suffer with another" and requires us to enter into the other person's pain. Only if we have bothered to walk for a while in another's shoes can we possibly begin to realize the extent of his suffering. Then, like St. Paul, we can "rejoice with those who rejoice and be sad with those in sorrow" (Rm 12:15).

Learning to be nonjudgmental in our listening requires a bit of practice since we have a tendency to be suspicious of anyone whose viewpoint differs from our own. It's a real sign of maturity to accept people just as they are, thereby realizing the wisdom of St. Paul's observation, "You together are Christ's body; but each of you is a **different** part of it" (I Cor 12:27).

My experiences with prayer groups have convinced me that everyone has a deep-seated need to be affirmed and accepted. Even those individuals who appear to possess great ego-strength bloom more openly in the powerful environment of loving, caring people. Jesus, with all his sensitivity, must have been aware of the faults in his disciples, yet he chose to concentrate on their attributes, enabling them to do great things.

Most of us are so overly conscious of our failings at perfection that we really need others to point out our good qualities to us. Of course, there are situations when a person needs to be confronted about certain attitudes or actions which are destructive to himself or to others, but even this can be accomplished through the gift of love. The teaching of St. Augustine to despise the sin yet love the sinner is a goal worth attaining.

A significant number of people initially become involved in prayer groups due to a crisis situation which prompts them to seek spiritual help. Therefore, most prayer gatherings devote a portion of their meetings to praying for the needs of others. When a group is small enough it is not uncommon for everyone to participate in praying over individuals for specific intercessions but this becomes unrealistic in large assemblies. As a solution to this problem, many groups designate prayer teams to minister on a personal basis.

The following are suggestions which may help to increase the effectiveness of such teams.

1) The prayer room should be reasonably quiet with a meditative atmosphere.

Distractions make it difficult to concentrate on prayer. Therefore, the place for refreshments and fellowship ought to be removed from the area designated for ministering to individuals.

2) If possible, the prayer room should be available before the general group meeting as well as afterwards. Many times people attend the prayer session for the sole purpose of receiving personal ministry and are, sometimes, too ill or too burdened to sit through an entire meeting. Providing an opportunity for people to obtain prayer before the meeting can also help to reduce the number of prayer requests at the end of the meeting.

3) Before they begin to minister, the team should pray over one another for the fullness of the Holy Spirit's gifts to flow through each of them. Team members may occasionally require prayer for a problem in their own lives

before they can reach out to others. It is also difficult to be a channel for the love of Jesus when we are harboring feelings of resentment or anger and we ought to be willing to rid ourselves of these barriers. This period of time can prepare us to be as open as possible to the presence of the Lord.

4) Whenever possible, people should be prayed over individually rather than in groups. This gives the team an opportunity to concentrate on the specific prayer request of the person. Jesus asked blind Bartimaeus, "What do you want me to do for you?" (Mk 10:51). It was surely obvious to the Lord that this man was blind but he wanted **him** to specify the need. I think many prayers go unanswered because we fail to define what we want.

5) The person being prayed over should be protected from the confusion of too many discernments, prophesies or

directions. Two or three team members are sufficient to pray for an intercession **unless** the individual seeking ministry requests the presence of friends or relatives.

6) A prayer team should never suggest that an individual discontinue medication, treatment or therapy. The healing love of the Lord also operates through these channels and they do not connote a lack of faith. Occasionally, the person seeking healing receives an inspiration to interrupt a particular course of treatment but this should be verified by his physician. If this inspiration really came from the Holy Spirit, he will confirm it through the natural order.

7) The prayer team should develop a sense of unity with one another which allows the gifts of the Holy Spirit to flow through the entire praying body so no one person dominates every situation. The Body of Christ can

function most effectively when all its parts are operating.

It is not unusual for a prayer team to be physically and spiritually exhausted after interceding for a number of people. We recall how Jesus knew the woman with a 12-year hemorrhage was healed when he felt "power had gone out from him" (Lk 8:47) as she touched the hem of his garment. Not only the power of the Lord flows through us to bless others, but also some of our human energy flows with it. For this reason,

8) It is advisable for other community members to pray for the team to be refreshed and renewed by the Holy Spirit. Any spiritual burdens acquired through ministering need to be released to the Lord who told us, "Come to me, all you who labor and are overburdened and I will give you rest" (Mt 11:28).

Prayer group members sometimes

become despondent when they have interceded for a healing and the person dies. They may look for all kinds of reasons to try to understand what went wrong. It helps to remind ourselves that even those people whom Jesus raised from the dead eventually did die. There is a time when our Father will call each of us to come home to him. When we've done everything we can to bring healing into a situation, we must leave the outcome in the Lord's hands.

Praying for needs of others can be a fulfilling and rewarding ministry even for those who are not yet healed themselves. The unselfishness involved in reaching out a helping hand can open up the door for great blessings. It is interesting to note how many of the recognized miracles at Lourdes, France, occurred while the person was praying for someone else to be cured.

I have two beloved friends who do not allow their physical handicaps to deter them from praying with others. Virginia Block of Libertyville, Illinois, and Amy

Landry of LaGrange Park, Illinois, are both beautiful channels for the healing love of Jesus Christ, although they have been confined to wheelchairs for much of their lives. God has given them a gift of faith which has influenced many lives and they avail themselves of every opportunity to minister to others. Sharing this faith has opened the way for the Lord to gradually bring wholeness into their own lives. The process has been slow but has encompassed every aspect of body, mind and spirit.

I cared for Virginia's physical needs for several years until we moved to Florida and I never failed to receive a blessing from her. She taught me to be patient with God when my prayers weren't answered as I wanted them to be. Through Virginia I learned the reality of the words of Isaiah, "For my thoughts are not your thoughts, my ways not your ways . . ." (Is 55:8), which helped to put my relationship with our heavenly Father into proper perspective.

Virginia and Amy have a deep devotion

to Jesus in the Eucharist and they receive Communion frequently. Amy is one of the founders of the Community of Living Waters, a charismatic prayer community which places a heavy emphasis on the sacraments and teachings of the Roman Catholic Church. It seems more than a coincidence that during the International Conference of Catholic Charismatics held in Rome in 1975, Amy's body was partially restored to health as she was receiving the Body of Christ at the Mass. Before every Communion we pray, "Lord, I am not worthy to receive you, but only say the word and I shall be healed." I have sometimes wondered what would happen if every person who approached the altar believed in the reality of those words.

Chapter 6

On Becoming "Little Children"

Jesus said, "I tell you most solemnly, unless you change and become like little children you will never enter the kingdom of heaven. And so, the one who makes himself as little as this little child is the greatest in the kingdom of heaven."

Matthew 18:1-4

JESUS TAUGHT US the necessity for developing a childlike nature if we want to be a part of the Father's kingdom. In every culture there are certain qualities exhibited by children which the Christian needs to emulate before he can know God's love.

To be childlike is not the same as being childish, a term which implies selfishness and immaturity. "The one who makes himself as little as this little child" is deliberately putting aside his own desires in order to respond to the Lord's directions in every aspect of his life.

Little children are spontaneous in their actions since they aren't complicated by reason and logic. They don't allow obstacles to hamper them from the goal they have in mind as every mother of a toddler can attest. Our eldest son, Chris, was just learning to walk when I took him into a department store one afternoon. His curiosity was aroused by an aquarium full of fish and, before I could stop him, the entire tank came tumbling down, water, fish and seaweed going in all directions. I thought the experience would slow down his explorations but it only served to increase his determination to overcome all barriers.

Children have a high degree of trust since they must be totally dependent upon the people around them to provide for their needs. They don't usually find it necessary to plead for the necessities of life because they assume others will care for them.

A healthy child is capable of giving and receiving large quantities of love in a variety of situations. Kissing, hugging and touching are normal to his life and he thrives in this type of open environment.

Jesus asks us to become like little children; trusting, loving and uninhibited, but we discover great barriers in the way. Living in the world has caused us to erect a wall of protection around our childlike characteristics in order to keep from being hurt. We tried trusting others and we encountered broken promises. We opened ourselves to love and to be loved only to discover insensitivity and pain. Acting uninhibited brought us admonitions to "grow up" and "act your age."

These life experiences have a way of suppressing the child within each of us, making it difficult to maintain the kind of free and open relationships necessary for spiritual growth. We can function but it requires a tremendous amount of self-effort.

I believe that the healing love of Jesus Christ can release our inner child. In fact, I think this is part of the message involved in proclaiming "liberty to captives" (Lk 4:18), which Jesus announced at the beginning of his ministry. Each of us has experienced numerous traumas which continue to affect our lives. These wounds may have occurred many years ago, and we have completely forgotten them, but the child within us never forgets anything. Asking the Lord to touch these painful experiences can be a big step toward entering into the kingdom of heaven.

A young man requested prayer because he was unable to feel joy in his life. He had received the baptism of the Holy Spirit several months before and had been granted spiritual gifts of prophecy and tongues but the process was sterile and automatic. We asked the Lord to heal his childhood memories of living with an alcoholic father who abused him verbally and physically and the change was instantaneous. Joy came flowing from deep inside him like "fountains of living waters'' (Jn 7:38), and he was really set free.

There is no way of measuring the amount of influence these negative experiences can have in our lives, but no one seems to be immune from painful memories. Even those situations which seem insignificant from an adult point of view can be devastating to our inner child.

I once prayed with a woman who had an irrational fear of the outdoors. She could not be outside for any length of time without feeling severe anxiety which made it impossible for her to enjoy a vacation with her husband and children.

I asked the Lord to touch anything in her past which may have provoked such a reaction and a rather simple episode came to mind. As a small child she was playing along the bank of a river and, oblivious to the dangers of the rushing water, began to wade into it. Suddenly, she became aware of shouts of alarm as her father scooped her into his arms, warning her to never go near the water again. Although many years had gone by, the intensity of that command continued to affect her behavior. I told her to recreate the scene in her imagination, this time bringing Jesus into the picture. She saw the Lord walking with her along that riverbank and, instead of instilling fear, pointing out the beauty of his Father's creation. I knew she had been released when, several months later, a postcard arrived from the Grand Canyon describing the marvelous time she and her family were having at the park.

Isaiah prohesied that Jesus would bear our sufferings and carry our sorrows to the cross. Not only did the Lord die for the sins we committed, he was crucified for the pain and sadness inflicted upon us as victims of this broken world and "through his wounds we are healed" (Is 53:4-5).

Since God will not violate our free will, it is necessary for us to invite him to enter into our hearts and touch any painful memories we have stored there. Even if we can recall nothing which might impede our spiritual growth, we can still ask the Holy Spirit to direct Jesus' healing love to any past experiences which may need to be touched. The Lord doesn't erase these traumas from our lives, but he transforms them so they no longer have the power to keep us in bondage. We can still remember what happened without negative feelings of fear, anger, sadness, guilt or pain.

Inner healing is like physical healing. It can be immediate, releasing years of suffering in one prayer, or it can be a process over an extended period of time. It will be a step toward wholeness whichever way the Lord chooses to work.

The following is a meditation which may be helpful in opening the door for this healing of the inner child:

Jesus, I ask you to enter into my heart and touch those life experiences which need to be healed. You know me so much better than I know myself. Therefore, bring your love to every corner of my heart. Wherever you discover the wounded child, touch him, console him and release him.

Walk back through my life to the very moment when I was conceived. Cleanse my bloodlines and free me from those things which may have exerted a negative influence at that moment. Bless me as I was being formed within my mother's womb and remove all barriers to wholeness which may have affected me during those months of confinement.

Grant me a deep desire to want to be born and heal any physical or emotional traumas which could have harmed me during the birth process. Thank you, Lord, for being there to receive me into your arms at the very moment of my birth, to welcome me onto the earth and assure me that you would never fail me or desert me.

Jesus, I ask you to surround my infancy with your light and touch those memories which keep me from being free. If I needed more of a mother's love, send me your mother, Mary, to provide whatever is lacking. Ask her to hold me close, to rock me, to tell me stories and fill in those empty parts of me which need the comfort and warmth only a mother can give.

Perhaps the child inside feels deprived in the area of a father's love. Lord, let me be free to cry "Abba," Daddy, with every part of my being. If I needed more of a father's love and security to assure me that I was wanted and loved very deeply, I ask you to hold me and let me feel your strong, protective arms. Give me renewed confidence and courage to face the trials of the world because I know my Father's love will support me if I stumble and fall.

Walk through my life, Lord, and comfort me when others were not kind. Heal the wounds of encounters which left me frightened, which caused me to retreat into myself and erect barriers to people. If I have felt lonely, abandoned and rejected by humanity, grant me, through your healing love, a new sense of worth as a person.

Jesus, I give myself to you, body,

mind and spirit and I thank you for making me whole.

Thank you, Lord.